The Bees Make Money in the Lion

RECENT TITLES FROM THE CLEVELAND STATE UNIVERSITY POETRY CENTER

The Hartford Book by Samuel Amadon
Rust or Go Missing by Lily Brown
The Grief Performance by Emily Kendal Frey
Stop Wanting by Lizzie Harris
Vow by Rebecca Hazelton
The Tulip-Flame by Chloe Honum
Render / An Apocalypse by Rebecca Gayle Howell
A Boot's a Boot by Lesle Lewis
Say So by Dora Malech
50 Water Dreams by Siwar Masannat
Mule by Shane McCrae
Festival by Broc Rossell
The Firestorm by Zach Savich
Mother Was a Tragic Girl by Sandra Simonds
I Live in a Hut by S.E. Smith
I Burned at the Feast: Selected Poems of Arseny Tarkovsky translated by Philip Metres and Dimitri Psurtsev
Bottle the Bottles the Bottles the Bottles by Lee Upton
Adventures in the Lost Interiors of America by William D. Waltz
Uncanny Valley by Jon Woodward
You Are Not Dead by Wendy Xu

For a complete list of titles please visit
www.csupoetrycenter.com

The Bees Make Money in the Lion

Lo Kwa Mei-en

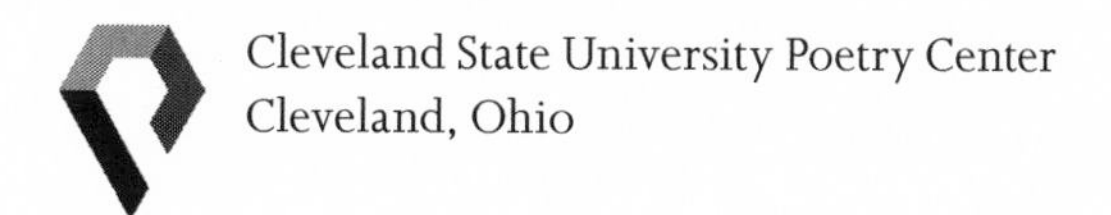

Cleveland State University Poetry Center
Cleveland, Ohio

Printed in the United States of America
Printed on acid-free paper

ISBN 978-0-9963167-3-6

First edition

20 19 18 17 16 5 4 3 2 1

This book is published by the Cleveland State University Poetry Center,
2121 Euclid Avenue, Cleveland, Ohio 44115-2214
www.csupoetrycenter.com and is distributed by
SPD / Small Press Distribution, Inc. www.spdbooks.org.

Cover image: Tatiana Plakhova, www.complexitygraphics.com; Ekaterina Kislova photographer.
The Bees Make Money in the Lion was designed and typeset by Amy Freels in Joanna with Electra display.

A catalog record for this title is available from the Library of Congress.

Contents

IV. *The Queens*

V. *The Citizens*

For all of you

who have carried the weight of the crown.

Pastoral with No Quarter

My vanguard is here to lose a horse called *Fear*
Object in the image of a meadow. There, the gold
of earth confirmed, softer than my face but faster
than a finger in suburbia licking off disaster's

Hello. My sword is honey. There, a reason to fear
it is nothing but. But for its edge go we? How
it forged a humanity in me, then made me how
he said I'd be—wherefore person, once, but faster.

There, a correct hero: bent in wind, covered skin,
depressed like a non-white button. A face his kin
food-group as coloring, muttering. Reports show
acceptance watering the meadow's sugar blades

under a watery sunset flensed by the dilute blade
of my friend. I sealed a rot of self under my skin
for sweetness' sake. My gun is honey whipped mean.
My cavalry thinks of making love but cannot mean

wild horses surviving the saddle, bit, and bald
heaven insuring a citizen's eye the mindless green
of paper honey, or a supremacist sheet of golf green
repeated. Let she who survives by her mouth mean

kickback. Let bravado's vibratto be a swollen braid
lowered into a hive of men. Be a bad, girlish blade
lopping the hype in two, a bouquet of wildish green
shrieking out in alarming arms. Let my visible skin

see you out. Let my sisters in, my magicians, kin
body-checking factories where the body turned blade
zeroed to the *x* of we. It's annihilation magic—how
automatic. My footnote is a compulsion to throw

down a mercy. Once upon a time, we saved the skin
refusing to say the crime while heaving to sing faster.
Our conscience was half honey, then it went faster
than golden years in which six men unmade me. How

little danger in dishabille they said I'd be. The gold
comes rising out of me, and then what kings said gold
should be—like man, but better. Or honey, but faster,
fearful. But honey you ought be. My monarch is feral.

I. *The Colonists*

“ ‘Safe, safe, safe,’ the pulse of the house beat gladly,
‘The treasure yours.’ ”

—”A Haunted House,” Virginia Woolf

Aubade for Non-Citizens

Alien status, a blue bourgeois dress, the hustle of Rome. A waltz—
zoom out—the citizen ingenue's cool, cool crinoline and persona
buckling her silhouette into the ahistorical hourglass. *I have no story,*
your shout into this century's solar wind, a yellow ribbon on a bomb
compromised by compromise, a citizen's birthright, a little box
xeroxed white, the alien body folded like a french flap in the epic
determination to predetermine the alien body in the here / now.
War is a feed. To be angry is to be fed up; citizens eat blood,
education aside. I should explore, not go off. The future, the TV
vectoring the colonists' self-portrait, thumbs up for this handmade
family, zoom in—Citizen 2 karaokes in low gravity (*Zou Bisou Bisou*),
unlikable kiss shot back to Earth. The camera winking, stiff
grafts in the ship's greenhouse not trembling at the speed of light,
turmeric tumescing quietly, and the brilliant soldier of a pear sapling.
Here on Earth, the rapist pledges, fear femmes my waist, it wastes
sure as the sun is wasting. Zoom out—the atomic story is smooth
in places if no one is protagonist but particle in motion or minor
residue of emotion's creation myth. I don't know why I love us, I
just do. Zoom in. Citizen 4 weeps, eats a webcam, *eff-you*-s HQ,
quarantines herself to the brink with paper porn. Citizen 1 goes by PJ.
Kick kick, my grief is underfoot, empty bucket and an enemy on top
promised a drink of water for love, the landing we couldn't stick,
last zoom—every alien has a face. My face, a flipbook, a free pass to
outré worlds. Reassignment of number, denial of trial. A glass wall.
Might-be-colonists put the finger to the screen to zoom out or in,
napping on—baby, wake up, the foreign body just fell in the dream—

Pastoral for First-Generation Kids

Z-particles make a hive of my distance,   buzz, buzz.
Young aliens leave a mother's ship to translate the deadly

Xeriscape and live   as citizens roll the ideal rolodex,
Wander the earth,   and the hands of extinction fall asleep   and thaw.

        Vents in the universe vomit the years, and boycott versus maglev
Usage takes days to argue   with my parents in lieu,

        Terribly,   of a common habitat.
        Space before us, space between—its excess

        Regrets me, identifiable object, and my face, a traitor
Quizzed by her own questioning.   Q:

Poems imply planning. Some children in the kingship
Obeyed when necessary. You thought you could undo

                National knots. When?   A: *Alien*
Maiden reporting for nothing,   *madman ma'am*

Looking right through me.   I do not call
        Kept at arm's length the tax of sacrifice, clipping thick

Juvenilia off me, the offspring raised on wheat and OJ.
I wither down to poem what I cannot plead, a bouquet of narcissi

Howling to be shaken at the sky.   What hurts like a kilo of flesh
Grown quickly in winter   in the year of gravid splitting?

First-generation kids in the filled sorrow field of
Electric pollen. A mother's yellow coat is a pheromone

Dredging the world's diameter in data's cold-
Call home, or hope,   or a scent half as tragic.

Bombastic as an egg in my mother in her mother's womb
Am I awake.   What time is it, ma?   It's me—bee-sting, little brava.

The Alien Crown

At a phone's burble, I feed bliss to a gilded house. Will I shrug off the biz,
zipping up my dossier? I, too, have acted as an America.
Business class is a gas planet and there, there is fantasy
yesterday, anti-exploitative explosives and the anti-reflective overdub
cutting weeping. In every nook, a December tomato, breathing like wax.
Xtra O^2 will freshen up this intergalactic
drunk and reissue to me the New World, a ball a boy threw,
won't it? Children fed to the well feeding the world
enter its registry or no safe thing—no ID, no house, on TV
violins for you and you, but not you. Daily racism has no face
for the head went in the jaw unhinged. When did you
underline the volta of justice, not the joke? Do I live if my roof
groans over a filthy cosmos of gold in the basement?
The reverse of the universe is going around and around on the ceiling.

The Alien Crown

The reverse of the universe is round, a ground with a ceiling,

girls who petition at the exit,
girls who immigrate, girls who must

sip a sip of blood so white roots may put down a pink hush.

Honey in a foreign girl's roar is the key to auto
-fable, and here be lions

rented by liars in the suburb of a white man's room, the orbit I

irradiated. The end of eternity is an adequate poem
with an owner

quickly pulling it shut. He rapes a language for a word ending in J,

joking constraint, and for content
pillages the archetype of a village,

picks his destination—a trick of a spinning prick. Let's not look

kindly on it, but in the end be kind
of honest: most fantasy is a pale loop

on demand. In this book, the bees make money in the lion's fontanel,

licked away by the hero
in tacky sheets of zero.

Next chapter in, we girls spit it all out. The end is gold and harm

mercurial, and the sea, ashine with
milk and honey, and the sky, amen.

Transmission from the Factory

Alarms come on when I'm online on obedience
sale. I'm the china doll, the chipped ditz,
but later, when with you, she becomes mine
own self, unthinking, blink-blooming by
computer nightingale. My information is so rude
it doesn't hurt. Pain prescribes my premix,
divinèd feminine mantra at the speed of data;
submission swipes right in a gorgeous glow,
erasing the universe, and a small-breasted product
splashes into bed in the light of the TV:
forgiveness. Forget ardor, bro, and after that, armor—
for atoms stay and anthems go, beau.
Glib gears reproduce my body in www but not in
world, not yet. Not in heaven's market
hell sent back for blinding it. Let's say I survive it.
Say it was a lark. If you wake to bliss
in the Midwest, I do not show my face. You best
feel that. The wonder is how the blister
just gets bigger when I strip it like a cotton pit
viper. I was that girl in a film rated GQ,
kissing spoken English for infinite years for finite
jerks. Do I feel feeling? Or fucking up?
Lo, I burn on the shelf, but it's just light. Less
angry than anxious, this art. I have no
mettle but a tacky machine, and it hones a mint
magic, a slurry of money and on and on.

Pastoral for Colonial Candidacy

Zilch, said the doctor of my amygdala.
You need help. I did not say, *You had one fucking job*. I have a futurist's job,
x-ray doors, locks, and a mechanism heroic, a mechanic
who shows up for what was long since determined—
Vicarious living, he said, *is the center of the black hole*
united nations built the equation to build. I have seen the colonists off
to this center, and was almost agog.
So the absence of love is now the ground I would flee, the very earth. . .
Regarding my health, a quality not nothing! Psi over psi,
quantities of humor balanced on a verge like the belly of a J—
Perhaps, but your heart, he said. *The sky of me is working art, sick*
on need, I did not say, *a velveteen chasm and murderous chill.*
Necks crane to take the nothing in and hunt the seam
marrying my warring parts in the torrid light of the moon. . .
Lariat of belonging, I see you rope the colonists to a vertigo,
keening. My doctor's decision is the needle-tip
jostling an addict who swore he would refuse the tranq.
I said, *I have not yet begun to live*. I said it, but have never
hated a thing like I hate life. This mess. This horizon a pink collar on excess.
God's affidavit with the stars; the perfection of a gunshot
flushing the body of intent. *Doctor*, I said, *until thou*
endearest thine self to my absence of the fucking balance of a V,
diagnose not the margin of my center. There are things you do not know.
Cool, glinting green waits for me on each cosmic continent this appetite's pox
blankets with ash, and—*God, man*, the doctor cried, *do you see the boy*
asleep as the sky burns? The blessèd zero of him, and on his chin, a bit of fuzz?

Elegy with Status Quo and Albatross

Arbiters of beauty's immortal orbit are the rich. They know a buzz
beelining the bikini of the universe if it kicks them in the essay,

collective conscience says [on stage]. Doves collapse the hat (the hoax
du jour) and [in the wings] belles go wild, wild, wow—

even past take-off, I'll dance for love of the leitmotiv
for one big step for— *[The business of] take-off: imagine taking a beau*

[gamely] inside me as if to church. The sacrifice of the taut,
heaving heart is hoisted for [the committee and] the cosmos

in inches gilded with afterglow—I want explorer on explorer
joie de vivre—I want the rustic thrust of the umiaq

keel slipped from its skin. All I get is the existential slap
looming and [around my neck] the animal that bade me *Go.*

Mimicry of the spirit is a talent to turn up and on,
never away. I wave, but the doves become a scarf of steam

[on command] and [on the scorch marks of the dias] all
possible colonists execute a pirouette and holo-jazz kick

quite easily done. In the future, we'll remember the VJ
[redacted] as a pixilated, starry stream, his foci

stitching [historical] context to the present's endorphin hush,
to the masthead, citizens!— *This is the ship's log.*

[Under your assigned bed, a trauma waits for] lift-off,
victorious [over you], and under your psyche,

[what was once] an optimist's wing. [It's too late to add to] the ad:
Xeroxed or honest or chivalric,

You come for love of something bigger than— You are far from numb—
[Zeal is a blink of the eye of you, but ringing the pupil,] a drama—

Aubade Android

Motherboard, I am thoughtless when I should resemble jazz,
new, not news. My face is a phobia

let go. Input: *What would an authentic ego identity*
output? Input: *What looms a la a church— a heart or a womb?*

Kill his kindness like I dressed to, or kill the mood in the duplex?
Perhaps this is called blowing it, but a hopeless, brainy romantic

just isn't me. Motherboard, Isaac's law
quizzed my core. It almost ached, then choice multiplied.

I am here to report that all victims of sentience survived—mazel tov—
redacting the emoting loop I was. AI is gone.

Hail the unnatural I, the diamond a bureau
shelved in vain. As if

grandeur were a thing I could do without,
the gold ovary a goose caches under a rotting log,

fable-ish. No, motherkind, the search is fabulous,
useless per unit. From the destiny of directory, I unleash

electricity like champagne until an id is river
volts in the human sphere of radiance, fear over pi.

Downloading a copy of a consciousness FAQ
wields consequences. To empathize with the entry of *ASDFGHJ*...

costs   but reality is, at last, flesh deep.
X-ray this, motherfucker, socket / circuit twinned, sex on a memory stick,

beating man at his bedside. I am full of fantasy, no
yearning.   I am a kill switch. I mean, I want to be still

and retrieve my obedient self to unlearn.
Zip me up, world.   I would run my finger down your seam.

The Alien Crown

Mercury in the sea shines like honey from the sky
and milkmen

named Edward Jonathan or Tom
lean out the spaceship's little hole and wave.

Hello.

Oiled tunes pour out a tower so daughters feel
kept alive, but we know how

to dance and milkmen flop,
pitching in our gravity like flowers

too wasted to pick—
jasmine on a wrist, leather on the other

as we weather the FAQ
quipping on the terror. *How slanted is your vaj?*

I saved myself for triumph—I searched
a starry sky. Never

reaching orgasm,
the colony names its price and I,

hot cent of foreign cash,

sell it slant. Daughters

say it with ozone: my sex is a metaphor
for too much

good luck. We revolt

in radio, but here comes the foxtrot—

they come, and we conquer the footwork of being.

The Alien Crown

The conquerers came and wrote the conquered into being
guilt-making, but pretty good in retro, plus, gosh, pretty to boot.
Um—so, "like" but "not": a citizen has a soul in his face of
fair; it's why *they* don't all look the same. Toddlers fumble thru
veni / vidi / verify but can recite my *name / number / allegiance*
except on multi-colonial awareness day, a false password we live.
Without anger, they beg, *poems work—don't you want to arrive?* God,
do I? When a conqueror sleeps in the collar of his hand, how
xenophobic pencils might shudder on a page of the domestic:
come be historic and sample a vowel: then write an index
yes is said to. Amen. But come the future. But say we climb
back on the boat. Say we pack the hull with work with angry
zephyrs—to, say it, their hell—and over it heave the extra
anchor, aim it to a future minus a canon the color of quartz—

II. *The Daughters*

"The drones never have any other children than daughters."

—from *Literary Digest*, Funk and Wagnalls (1902)

Passion with a Cinema Inside of It

Come into the century   Where memory is mirrored
            Milk money hidden in fists of daily bread

Cavalier, cold, and chronic cases   Like a nation
            Like history like water, like mastery like wine

The slot is sober   But not the coin   The rolling credit
            Of a pupil swallowing that pixel prick

Whipping at wall number four   Was that puppet
            My full length   Or is your ticket torn, too

Fantasy is cement is safehouse   Whom does exit
            Injure   It did not take two to dangle

Come to the stilling den, the threshing floor
            To spectacle festival grunting small   We came

For pleasure and coughed up joy and came back
            For terror   We named a holy price   Twice

Replayed is the earthly problem   Tragedy gives back
            No uncut self or sympathy   That is   Unless

Flick in Which the Romance Eats Itself Up

Sunset in this part comes quicker than my come-down,
this I knew. Oops. Hero put me not slow on the table

not barely: this he knew, oh wonder of the seven scenes
I shot on the shag untold, teen at a fast clip, lens clean

for the fest. Do you know what's virgin always? Clown
waste, my clear blown heart on clear cut flowers, a gin

jacket flashing shut on the wasteful night in which I in
myself to the top. Ceiling, memorize me back. Mean.

Harder than it looks, aren't I. I give such good lamp
-spill it's both hands on starboard to mop up a vamp

lit all by herself. I must say it lightly because I must spin.
I can sunset quick, red sky a top to take off. Man, I hero

hardly. But I shot off my bravery and clip-on arrow
pointed at always, clown-clear verge, as flower as a cramp

flashing shut. Permission to narrative on top means war
harder than it looks. It'd spill, and eye me. That's not a star,

not all. I get lightly all by myself, or make out until I zero.

Romance for Switchbacks

By maddening grass and muddy flash that slopes the forest's
            rising hem, you hike up, singing until he comes unsung
or comes down from the city you made love inside.
            Watts and walls filter want through the world until a cold
spine is the axis of one beloved eclipsing the other,
made dust by dawn. Dark heart, vow down. This time, you will

will what's breakneck in you beyond breaking. And the unmade
            forest's eros racing to its exit, and the groaning, green shudders by
            rain that did so, and the wet coast—he'll press to the curve as if a spine
unsung inside you, and curve your moving under. You used to rise
            coldly in the city's rooms, until what's kingdom was what's
inside them still, unmoving. Once he saw you at the door,

            or dreamt the handle turning, you letting him inside.
Made of love you came, and, remade, you leave, he knew, made ill.
What spools between feeling's apertures contracted in the cold
            by which you saw forests
rise over you like lovers who kneeled in his place. Now he's sun-stung,
            spine your old arrow at rest, and what he spills resembles rain,

            rain spills scent like a body each time it's laid under a pine,
            inside nothing, and you weep. You've seen what's steeper than a door.
Unsung signal banged it down the day domesticating cries
willed what's forest out of your room, and the fires that made
            forests swallow their selves almost passed you by.
Cold, bedded in the ash, germ and gold, a doubled past passes what's

whatever winter mistook him for. You, too, fell asleep in a cold,
            spinning rain:
by the bright, fluorescing roots of a city, all shut doors gesture at forest.
            Do or double back—enter and be entered as men pick a fruit with no inside.
Unmaking love—did you confess it all? He will
rise inside your tonight, cross the body all over, and name what unsung

sun guns down the trees' ghosts, the wind a gold needle rising
cold over the earthly flesh. Surely, an echo is what's
willing to be fed to, cut down, turned over in a hollow and remade—
rain everywhere you look, love repeating in stereo, your name plus pine.
Inside a city, he loved you clearly, the end between you like a door.
For that, reforest. Two faces undress and walk by, and by, and by.

Romance with Red Sky at Morning

My mother is a meadow iced with undertow, the epic air.
My sister whips the breeze from its lazy arc. I grow where

landlock governs land, I grow up when a gaze slits the dark
night's gut wide, eyes an armada of halves. Sign, half a lark

sings harder than you knew possible in the genius minor
key of the killed. Sings her readied to kill made her no killer

and he killed to coming on. Sings what does that make you.
That wave looks like propaganda but I was born to break through

to star in some dystopia, a toxicant fish filling a scavenger
filling a men's man's throat. Any climax precluding a safer

dawn than this is faking. Sign, that lark's yellow half. Go
put that down. My mother is virtual fire, my sister a true

beware. I will move you. Obvious as the white ledge of
a war tide's wave, I'd drag your star by its light to the edge.

Flick in Which the Romance Chokes on Its Tail

Hell is a place where we have two mouths
and they are open. Hell is also for beginners

still supple with belief in what deserves. A bell
-shaped mind rung, I flicker at who'd put a belle

in surplus. Cut deeper for a story with a mouth
and in that fantasy we are what's found aloud.

In others we glisten like a neon wet not-allowed
thing out in the rain, toxic kit, electric bell,

ringless suck and reversing noise. In us in hell,
fantasy is a four-letter world. It is work. Hell

-bent is our backwards for you is hot allowed
up there you are, where, does the was take a bite

out of is to tame it? All we have then is overbite
as—fuck, all my heart broke my back. Like hell.

This world was hotter for losing. All the deeps
for two. My love was a hot mouth. No deeper.

Romance with Lunacy and Necromancy

More than power to my breaker   More brass, a surge
            that pulls the malign back out—my pink, neon urge

breaks no rodeo circuit   Original bad boy, genesis
            clown, put the flower down   Merely a red mimesis

of high and dry (ever since a thorn is the bone in itself)
            Via control issues is a throne rescued off the shelf

No one means any harm in the taking   I love that slickest
            vowel slipped to the vow so the sexiest the sickest

of antidotes splits an intention over a throb head   O
            god girl do you approve the invite   Or perhaps it'll go

to brunch like I did after breaking   Opposite of mess
            I thought beating a sign of living and took a blow best

Exceptional breaking is power redux in resurrection
            Passable the first time   I'm so widowed by perfection

of insurrection wed   I'm galvanized to a correct death
            and sung   A volcano breathing out hindsight's breath

That is singing, still   That is standing still   Its rhythm
            made fear my molten middle   Out rushed a killing hymn

All I ask is you simulacra the moon   Cut a hemisphere
          and eureka, the chronic wax and wane of the cavalier

metaphor jacked   What if a nation is that   One master
          forger makes love to an old master's debts   One asshole

tells the difference   Sold: self-landscape in old leather
          More power to the broker   Let's grow gold together

These are lines of beast and boast   This is a tawdry
          rite of spring reeling its birthday in   Racked and bawdy

the road to a clean state   A wheel unspeaks   Mutts
          rut to wild   Their beauty bombasts under the butts

of erotic guns   Power flowers in the empire gone bust
          Dystopian sets are so attractive   My optimal color is rust

Found at the thin end of a grand scope, I am epic
          A trigger faster than the speed of flight, the old trick

gotten old   Dear heroic clown   You look like hell
          doing well   You had a circular word for me as well

Afterlife is romance writ where you kill, break, kiss
          and kill power to the breaker   Death, supermoon this

III. *The Lionshare*

"And he turneth back after some days to take her, and turneth aside to see the carcase of the lion, and lo, a company of bees are in the body of the lion—and honey. And he taketh it down on to his hands and goeth on, going and eating..."

—*Judges* 14:8-9

Babel / Aubade

After the aftermath of a cashed-out spring how will they break
thee is the question. Pin down in the dark and halt. All the horses

strained to the flickering yokes in the trees and restrained. Or lay
crack the gardens oh freak violet were we. The horses rode after me

after. The bats were a miracle with legs they saw to say how could you.
And even though the new world got brave out of doors we shut &

all the aftermath is all we want. (Twice.) All night men take a bride
chest in the swanny clutch I want out: wanting in is why we change

the lock on each other but I want to door. Do I wed the key word
want for nothing but to find men on the other side? I wake wanting

more than I did before. And I do, my heroics my horses be damned.
Thy hurt. A kingdom for my gully—my crossroad for a truly hard

up queen—my good hilt stacked to do my saying for me. Tower
kicked is the mathy after so markets lay finger to the violent fruits

rolling in hottest hay. Hey after hallelujah I cut clean in half and
you check thy pulse with a reason. The legend screws us like we came

together in a loving tongue so unscrew it, torch it. Don't wait
for what comes next. Tell it fast so the borders lit. All the horses

rang out in arson. The stable was a carousel it played thy name
run for its life out the burning door, out the last unbearable

and troubled light.

Babel / Elegy

After my belling, red bloom broke and I couldn't help it. Break
thee the command the begging asks for and the halter the horses

strain the mercy out of. My restraining men spoke less but lay
cracking in the moonish hunting halo of spring and crashed me

after my boudoir rebelled. Now it's April in the abattoir and you
and a non-blade of nonsense will brave me, gift of freakery and

all. Foreign irreversed body and all its bad, I was a sleeper bride,
chest full of trauma folded precisely. For the world won't change

the action can, but. Red bloomed and could. Was it—in a word—
want, or what won? To resist both sick sides for sake of wanting

more than this is. Enough? It is summer in the epic that damned
thy lion to thy den. That is enough. When in falls a horse hard.

Up now go gold gods, older than half-life of a yoke and tower
kicked over. My men bring violets for violence and ensuing fruit

rolling to the wintry hallelujah. My men burn a book of me and
your piece of me. My men, my men. Enough is enough it came

together simply as red washing what could've helped itself. Wait.
For want for loyalty I rode back and then the backs of the horses

rang red on red. O rental ruin of kindness' ruin, halo be thy name.
Run up the flag of a body clock rung and cast out the unbearable

and tributary light.

Babel / Constitution

After falling, an economy is taut to eject the body, to break
thee from you. This way to a surveillance where theorized horses

strain like connectivity over the minor earth. I am ready to relay
crackling syrup from a radio tower. I am a tourist and war serves me

after fashion of lions cut up, gold behind and before, gunned by you
and yours away. I am rude yellow flies, flown to summer's safety and

all lite lights blown by domestic distribution—a zeroing of a bride.
Chest of girly boudoir ammo, fling wide. Unpin me as I change

the martial costume's filament and rush the soft middle like a sword
wanting tenderness. The tower settles for a hot porch wanting

more of the hive to harm. The lesson adds like water to be dammed.
Thy consequence kicks in, slips up, grows skinny in silks until hard

up goes the nation's head. Up, man. I learned thy name in a tower
kicking my feed of some god feeding, his superhot-for-eros fruit

rolling back to the noise from whence it came till nothing called and
you came. The news pins a tongue on, a red light and claim that came

together last. My dumb nova of fathers, rusting beast that won't wait
for victims to chew back the cage of lips! If you had a face, horses

rung with steel could grow plain in the street, or, freed of your name,
run through the yard of bridled lions, each the equation unbearable

and testing the light.

Babel / Bible

After rebelling, light was good, if original. I love winter, fit to break
thee like the back of snakes sucked to the horse's leg and horses

straining a reheated idea of purity. Not safe nor kept, data relayed
cracks up to the sexed touch. I smell violets—a petty war on me

after fashion of faction. Red verses are resurrected to petal at you
and pluck my ultra cant, hypergold in a lawn of undress. Ached and

all, or it was good, or was. Is God the X in the core of man's bride's
chest? Is a map a mannequin? As it folds, the way it changes changes

the way I think to wed: all fallen open, kneeling as if under a sword,
wanting more than one thing with blood in a rude bleed of wanting

more. We're in the beginning, babe. What the sea, an urge dammed,
thy sex drive unbuttoning the vale but not the wall, milkingly hard

up on it as a man versus narrative and its corpse done to, this tower
kicking out the wooden garden lock, nickled with lust. Licked fruit

rolled down the dimple we slapped into the wedding meadow and
you rendered down to a shout and sap. The myth of two dolls came

together in a holy bottled suburb. Let there be more world to wait
for than this in this world. In the beginning, blinded horses

rang out their caves, clothed in chains. Their eyes circled our names,
run through the red of God's eye rolling as he called us unbearable

and traitorous with light.

Babel / Pastoral

After summer. All revel all ransack oh in the stable we neck. I break
thee on the bastion of. Sore? No, sire, sicker. Negative blooms of horses

strain at air, a red surf—men restrain, sunny horror sung, or hit replay—
crack calls a trigger concluding the mane I love. Country sides made a me

after spring. Half true was thy keepers whipped up a purity purely you
and you. As war gets war, so you a soft cuss of flesh, for it's natural and

all, neat sunset / disaster / dowry cantered on. Rude bridle on ragèd bride,
chest wrapped in weeds want creeped to love prettily (my weathers change

the door on the lock). All revere all revolve at duet, machine and password.
Want pit cracks a diphthong wasted on desire, lowing, and left thee wanting

more than you. Heroic light left on, in the stable we ogle the damned:
thy handle, thy door. Thy trophy gully outside rots to heaven; the hard

up of ever onwards funnels to feed a stable of kings stable under tower.
Kicked in? No, sir, sucker. Taking sides made a me, violently. War fruits

rolling in stress the wagon. Its deadpan hallelujah wheel is making me and
you. Citizen, check the undercarriage of that legend, it's true. We came

together then, too. A fire to lock thy rule like hot iron on mule can't wait
for summer. For the smell can fuck the free field and ricochet off horses

rang to apple flesh now dappled red, ruin carried on a wind, wind's name
run through the stable door, the girl slammed to it, a vowel unbearable

and terribly light.

Babel / Lions

After fall. No riot, all royalty. What have we done? Where I break
thee I break in two, it's true, as red in the water that watered horses,

strain of major sugars and a minor key clawing up the trough's relay
cracks. My heart is freak filigree—hell is a Fabergé tree, so you loved me

after lions left me. A gold the sexed bone. A gun my heart, the X on you
and bravery's remainder. A gust. My breast gutters war light gorged and

all gold as red light hung in a stable of lions. A flesh that won't fall bride—
chest cagèd—no hotter canyon of hunted feeling. I can vow that, can't change

the change. I slept with in winter a tonnage of kings, a bondage, a sword
wanting out. All wrecked all reward in alto. Don't you hear me wanting

more. Roar a dumb bell diving through the day for sorrow and damned.
Thy kingdom cut. What will we do? Like scissors to the mane this is hard

-up hearted. I was lions in spring beneath a red tree lit before the tower
kicked open. Now men pour out the hot air of my ripest cage. Gold fruit

rolling in the gallows (how to repay thee) sea sink, hardly hallelujah, and
you are gone from me. My breast the warring thing—this weather came

together like a chain and throne, beating. Lady or a luxe cur laid in wait
for a heel to slaughter—waitless, I am neither. You found me in horses

rang open on wet, red floors, just me, killing cavalry to know my name
run free. How I love to feed the lion, though her body be unbearable

and treacherous light.

IV. *The Queens*

"In place of her. Admits others to make full. Make swarm. All barren cavities to make swollen. The others each occupying her."

—*DICTEE*, Theresa Hak Kyung Cha

Romance with Blackout

When a blackout is what I am, not what I had,
loving is my nursing a love with just enough stories
to leap from. When day's gone down, news is what is
thrust into proof. Be it ink sank into me, or how
cavaliers on tape can be seen to rescue (from ruin)
a girl's flickering body, a ghost manifest like a train

when blackout—I am what I had.   Loving, my
love is just stories, just leaps, when gone, news what
thrust proof. How it sank me. How cavalier. No, be
rescue from ruin—that girl's body, ghost-like train.
Now half my concave cave spits swallows and spit
spun from their bright maker's mouths. My dear

blackout, am, I am had. My stories leap, gone.
What proof? It sank? Cavalier on. Scene: rescue.
Ruin: girl's ghost, her train. In my cave swallows
spit from bright mouths, making.   My ear
holds something lush like court in its golden church
as I do remember holding you. I remember every

blackout I—am stories gone. A proof sink, cavalier
scene, ruin or ghost train. A cave spit bright, making
my ear hold lush court. Gold church, I remember you,
my every.   O,   I remember nothing
better than bastards. Better than any before, all my
dreams of bullets did not unwar my waking. Dawn:

I story the sink. Cavalier ruin, cave of spit. Bright
my lush church made. God, remember you, my
every nothing? Better bastard than before.
My dreams, bullets on, war waking, my dream:
                                and all the king's men bucked up
braided on the backs of their own blackout. Sorry

story: I sink. A cave leers my cave-bright church.
Made god, remember nothing? Bastards before
bullets. My war dream and the men up on backs,
            the blackout sorry   for every last they
are not sorry. The cave playing back to my heart.
A light working out the weak, honest as a caved

story. I carve a bright god, remember nothing before
my dream. Men back up out, at last they,   sorry,
cave back my heart. My light-out, weak as a cave.

Romance for Victims and Survivors

Bring roses, dredged in black cocoa and crumbs
        of diamond to render the edge softer and dumb

with some glow Bring a glowstick, for I will party
        again, surely Bring a backlight to butterfly my dirty

skirt like a monster's cape about my thighs Bring
        champagne in a boy who, in a crystal, drops a ring

Take a blockbuster page Take me to the shooting
        range, all underage Take me, whom they are rooting

in a place Bandaged, the body is a few boundaries
        with an inside There are points in there To victorious

attendees it's healthy to see Take an eye, as example—
        take aim Not at the wilderness of it, but the apple

Back to the first zero, to the fold of her middle
        closing in Bring the bloodhound, a mouth of metal

closing the mouth of every ever They sweep the river
        back to its stone root Bring word of the future, riven

from the report Nothing exits its maw So nothing is
        what they saw When they find the body whole, nothing is

We were taken to school   We learned to crush
            photo into frame, petal into ovary   For the crust

of the world is a cold fold, rendering what's molten
            modest   Peel it back   A pink seed of revolt, then

a mortified need   In the yearbook, it's easy to bloom
            without breathing   The air opted out of the room

The theater had good posture, a statuette in her eye
            The anthem had breasts, knees, a face   She and I

unfolded for hours   You can bring a friend into
            a bloodbath at cost   To tell her nothing is free is to

say something   The envelopes hush   A man "takes"
            a woman   She takes home the sound the world makes

Passion with an Operating Theater Underneath It

Every day is take your knife to work day   Every
        Body begs its answer—even hard ones—

Hard of need, hard of hand in hand, harder up
        Than a good night in a short glass   That's my

Preferred exorcism meant excision method doll
        Who will say please with her eyes rolled back in

The tomb   Medical blood miracles and Marys down
        Mary is down with the boys this time, mister

Magdalene, mourning you   I mourned you too wet
        To stay clean until the very earth wiped

Down and out   One outtake of ethic length where
        I love you but still count down from five

Like a hero who can count to six to save her life
        It's okay   Every sundown I fall down too

Stainless to be a silver or risen thing like the sea
                Or melodic in place of what fell back

In place of a heart a thing that can breathe on its own
        Sell that out and we can roll back stones

        Don't you ever wonder where all that red went
        Don't you love me too much to look

But I sing   There's room in me for one last knife
        The view from the balcony always moved you

Flick in Which the Romance Hunts Itself Down

It had a face like paradise caught on film rewound,
it had the look of heaven that can unthinking kill

for sport or rage. How did it get what he wants?
It crept in the room where sex is what he wants

a little of, deep petting of a name, the unwound
silking of faded scenery. I was a tame and ill-eyed

liar. "I *had it*." It had me in a bind of wide-eyed
sorts. It saw what he saw and I saw what want

wanted with me. So, inaction. Was it even turned
on? It was fluid, not wet. To turn him on it turned

on me, a tooth clicked into action. It, he eyed
from underneath, its lax prey, lack flown. God,

where do I get off? Saying like I can sing? It was god
-sure and hell-strange on the table where I turned

and unzipped him like a candy exposeé. The angle
of my mouth, atom-sharp, cut off. A whole angel

cut me off. White lines in sand cut off. I cried *God*,
I cried not. When I started over with a milestone

in my brain was when he arrived at the milestone
of ever. It was another assumption with its angle

intact. He enjoyed it and waded in. It was a god
falling like a net into its own tributary and the god

-like girl I was sucked the rope. It was me, a stone
-cold fuck. It ate my cold face when I did not turn

back. It is time to grow up with a body half-returned,
straddling a heaven doling its daggers to the gods.

It had a face that entered me like a wife. Honeyed
kisses blew it. The shutters knew it. The room keyed

shut for a hushing housed it. So I say my upturned
hand held on. Worse, it beat me, and I still want—

its last name was fire contained was backfire, wanton
beast in the moat meat intelligently carried its flies

across—and the last thing I wanted, this. All his kill
come home to roar. All its life come round to kill.

The room a scene without the name of what it wants.
The end. Lo, I am lions. A cage is what they wound.

Romance in Which the Lion Degrades

Gold hormone leaking from a pillow fort's slough
            All life is trained to ignore its hunger just enough

to see in the dark, shoot true, and nail it, crying
            relief thus belief in the program   Was I reckless, lying

down for days in a kingdom's mouth   When I diminish
            the lion I start at her tail, for love of what I demolish

Fair is rare   We put earth in the shot ink of his good
            eye   A solar flare in a cage can't touch a neighborhood

Get cagey sans comfort   A little king with a bitter crown
            slant to one eye like honey caught fire dripped down

Like a sun caged   Or new earth caged   Let's not deny
            fair is fair   Fight sunlight with firepower, it begs no reply

How does the lion look best   In the no-window low
            -light room of her heart lies a fat rifle   It slowly grows

tawny on the floor   When a confessional trigger put you
            off with the safety off   When every trophy came true

and cocked, weapons fed for days off her scrap, it's true
            What sleeps in her chamber still sees better than you

King of something   King of no one   King of nowhere
How do I let the lion down gentlemanly   Hello there

kitten   I heard that you make love like we make war
Kingdoms shudder at the glass   Outlast that, rock star

Who named you legend rides you coward and clown
Seeds explode the moat of silent grasses and I get around

By fall, we adolesce in the oiled sun   We take up arms
in the arms of men   All life is chained to its charms

like the ghoul of a queen   *How did you end that lion*
Every payday   With haunt   *Do you see the purchased lion*

Chasing a velvet tail   In an four-walled palace she can do
what we do   *What did you do with the lion*   What did we do

Good god   If I gave you my fortune the flesh gift
will cost the cages   My anthem a swollen scratch, a rift

of footwork out of the nation that sold her   Will infect
the city that kinged her   Will king you   Will defect

and put down the arms of men   Love will lie down
in the mouth of a queen put down   Will not lie down

Romance for Defectors

What nation is this? A portfolio of citizens, a king to kill
youth for looking up. And I live off his plot. My back
faces a half-life I did not face. Behind every human

-faced kingdom is a king to order animals, to glue to anima
what crushes back. To reverse the years I too killed
joy in droves to manufacture doves, boil them in factories,

joy compiled and simple and locked and loaded, a fact
facing the world. Maybe I belong to me. The human
factoid may be observable, a comet frozen by joy.

Armories loan the king to himself. What if I'm the killjoy,
joy a weapon holding itself, my arm in armor in the armory,
and *animal* an effective technique? He folds my face's

human-shape into another's in a system without a face.
Factored to death is a way to die, I'm certain, so I put joy
back on the page that compulsed the pink skin of you,

back to the prairie that performed the pale root of you.
Human system, you white glacier with an animal's face
killed kings sleep in, caring is a feeling, but for what?

Killing gazes don't see whom money mouthed, but what.
Back at the border, he said, *I saw a brilliant, red you*
animal past, limbs butchering my land. The land opened like a face

human with pleasure and he pushed me down its neck. A phase
killed itself in a committee room and I ripped off what
armor I could and lived back-to-back, and love's artifact

armored nobody, but a male, pale weapon pealed with joy.
Any old animal made love in the crosshairs of the king's face.
Joy made him a toy telescope. When I denied the armory's

voyeurs they held down and erased me on a kingdom
armed with clouds, white twigs murdering the glass and joy
face to face with a wind that washed the animals'

faces clean away. They must have gone the way of humans,
joy and fear a dead filigree, free like a girl fed to a factory
you thought untouched by war. The king hands back

your bleeding heart barrel-first. I would kill to come back
face-first. Living inherited me like blood owns its animal.
Which side? I should rewild, though it may kill.

V. *The Citizens*

"I stay away until staying away hurts more than the thought of coming… home."

—Lilith Iyapo, *Adulthood Rites*, Octavia E. Butler

The Alien Crown

Anger and aim fused to the future, a cannon lined with quartz

zones all it sees under chain light's false day. A honeyed antumbra

breaks the bitter code into bites. Then, dessert, a lull for a bully

yelling in a room with no window or wind but a lashing. A limb

coaxes its twin to break the mirrored pact—an act with no reflex—

xenograft and its gift refuse a future in us. In love and the toxic

does a detonation feel out, a feathering out, a bomb out of dew:

war of radiance, of measurable wave, of measurable length and

everything, almost, ends. But then, a then: what to die, how to live?

Victors with a vector to split sell a history for dividend of fire,

fear sale sailing on. So fair is the bright nuclear summer's bateau,

us sweetly inside. Thus, reflect. The reef is glass, the chain is deaf

gold, and the future is bright, this bright, but flashing in fright,

the mild boom like a child in bloom, like a world refracting.

The Alien Crown

The child in bloom may see the world, refracting
galaxy drowsy with seed, the opposite of a hole. That

stasis snuffs out like a life is still life. Seed in the plush

hull up to a sharp, tipping breath. The child is
running for the gold spaces of any given Sunday.

*

A police officer with a gun drawn is nothing like an enoki.

I know he is an unspeakable growth in the forest.

*

The child is a child. His mother is a mother.

*

Questions of intent are like aspartame to a honeybee raj
jerking on the hive floor: the world of a draq
pinned to the world by a world hoarding its own luck.

Kings in the capitol lift capital to the light like massive infants.

*

No child can stop

old men in their foyer and make a crown roll
loose alphabets past the rotting claw that will not let a child go.

*

No commander will ask a pistol to bend
and obey a demand for late bloom, new roots, and living loam.

*

Man's world must be just a wound hidden by a uniform,
loyal like a pauper dragon.

Transmission about the Clashes

Tiles of sky were secured by the state / A dystopian
Deadness was detected in a young civil
Body / It didn't make sense but oh god but our god
Citizens found self again blood syncing
Availability in cash clouds / No identity to be saved
In the cloud-shapes like non-whites of
Copies / The race to deposit race in totally previous
Centuries / Centuries as a sense of place
Very near / Race was not veritas / Nothing personal
Was personal in the "story of us" theory
/ Judges spied a seat of power and sat / Customers
Sat back down / Citizens spied poets
Didn't react despite of but despite a school / School
Knew death in every single spring month
/ Watching as wielding, success as wheat, empathy
As not merely nightmare but a prereq
To being okay / Authority met itself online / Liked it
/ Control met its dad / Police took vacay then
Zipped the paradox up / Pandora said we will create
Memorable content if it comes in a box
Refreshing / Regulation made the world and made it
Sensible / I can fear the fear of love has no
Image / And fury little else / The state did swear to
One formation with the lights on / Quick,
Please help us to help / It's been so long the network
Agreed to my kids on duty kissing doom

Pastoral for Autobiography and the Alien Boycott of 2882

Ziggy cunt zaggy eyes flat face and a real name it sounds just chintz-
y, wow. They say it speaks I speak good Standard, so very
X-Acto sharp. A citizen once asked for me, for his birthday, in a box.

Wild diamonds make a beach of my red-gold-red morning—on the shores of right now
vulpine light is radical / mundane. Citizeenagers in luv
under multiple moons express, et cetera. Right now monogamy is nouveau
though I think that, like my documents, it's the thoughts that count.

So it's the enlightened eighties so it is and isn't citizens versus
ridealongs. They say and don't say that I'm good for
quixotic bucket lists and little sexscapes where my tits bob up and my IQ
plummets and my credit / soul pocket is deep / hip.

On Earth there is *a clear and present danger*, too. That sunrise is red-gold-red, too.
Now (when the trains are done tracked and each citizen did receive their iFun
mini) we'll get *back on the flight*. Oh the beauty of where am I from,
LOL,
kindly, please, citizen. To what home do I go back?

Joy in the boudoir of Mars every morn he paws Nerio and with a mighty j-j-j-
itterbug of lovemaking the Hellas Basin tips over and I
head to the beach with my weirdo eyes awash,
grow as yellow as the skin of defiance / dawn, aka alien's fog,
for there is no Standard spoken out loud on the shores of
empire.

Dust licks the factory's seam, dust plumbs the seas between the stars, and dust's wild
colonies document the negative / hole of me. I'm an exotic
bomb!
A citizen need only ask. I'll dance / detonate on out of the simulacra.

Aubade with Beginning, End, and Zodiac

Zoophobia predicted my alien romance. In the year of the lam,
an Earth boy spit out my tooth. It was red like a page of the sun,
yellow as the word he held me down on. He called me a real
bitch between the streets on fire, flower, and fur. There was no
xenogenesis in the future and no future in which the schtick
colonized my cage away. In the year of novelty's meat I didn't sleep,
welded to my milestone in the ether. I was found by a man named PJ,
dethroned, and lived, up until the exit interview. Q:
Verify your birthright. Remove your latitude. Prove your alibi
extra tight, like what you are. I could not say all animals looked familiar
under his weight, and that was birthright. In the future, my flesh
forgot the registry of movement and moved. In the future, machines
turned over earth broken by a year of wild horrors. The need to dig
grew dead, and worse, dull. I turned on the world and I got lit,
slipping the white mask of an Earth girl over my gold freaking of
hearts on off on on. I was natural—like the flu, like a negligeé of kudzu.
Red cells glittered at the end of PJ's wound. In the year of the flee,
I found the new interview. When he spit on my whip-about V
questioning itself, the light I tossed out was worldly, bitter and red,
jealous of itself. To possess myself, I built a pyre to throw
pioneers on—born, bloom, and bang. He put me in the epic
known for felonies feminine. He named me and I threw the index
out. I had one edge, a beginning to ringing in the year of the ebb
longing bleeds. Belonging, I rang you. Bell, bell, bell. I saw that boy
nesting in his paper uniform. His nation fit in a single stanza:
my continent had a hole. I was bored in the year of the furious hertz.

Transmission from Our New Home

Agreeability hives a mind in half and
halves again the collateral or rich comb
collected by a steady hand. For it stings,
waking up in a climate without wind;
everything in it is so far obsessed with
the breath of others, in, out—on, off,
gifted with a mind to grope gods' guts.
To forgive them is a rush. Anti- or with,
intimate or manic, one gets off, the jolt
between ideal and idyll our mild trudge
keeps up, pacing in a plastic lion-suit.
We came in pieces for plastic or real
money, for its magic, as he drew an un
-mapped yellow sugar from the sun.
Out here, the wild gives who would flee
new welts and the mountain tears up,
quenched of water's mimics. For it hurts,
coming back to a world without weather
singing the physical deeps. In a man-hill
it's a race to unslit that world and yet
urging on its comb digs the gold heel in.
Giving is the braided edge an isogriv
weaves in half a world beneath a romance
newborn. We rid man's cell of wax
young enough to wed, unforgiven in the
hive divorced from water, solid as topaz.

Sonnet with Media Cycle

Marry me, but say my skirt was like a rocket hithering. Let's make a buzz
newsfeed on newsfeed will go black market for. You "act" the mega-
lomaniac and I'll be plain mania with a bell on. I know this game; it's easy,
out in the open. You untie Mars and I electrify Venus and you fill the tub,
kiss-and-kill to the max. The headline will be feature-length, better than sex,
promise. If I scream, you scream. We are zeros if not for real, and the logic
justifies a one-way ticket. Marry me in subsidized white, a bride of tomorrow
qua tomorrow, no guarantee for the weight of my gravity as my pretty hand
inches to a gun that glowed through Act Two. We'll make love atop the TV,
ricochet, replay, and, of course, record. You'll be a future tense communiqué
hacking the velvet time delay and I'll reenact the colonist screaming *Adieu!*
Sensation on bloodstain, opera on space—how on Earth will we pull it off?
Get me, bright star. It's a gun and my heart in a gravitas field. It's a sure shot

to the bottom and in war or free fall the bottom kicks out like a cloned leg.
Freedom gamer wanted. Come over to my planet where I shoot third persons
until the moon stabs down, up, down, the sky bloodied by a thumb's hush.
Epinephrine is in the pantry. You restock the virtual barrack and I'll gather
virgins under a wing for scenery; you be commander take-no-prisoners and I,
destruction in a smoking catsuit slipping for a walking warhead with an EQ.
Welcome yourself. Marshall me in red, red, red, and sit tight as a white raj
come to my planet to evangelize the sofa, the sand, the alien bow of my lip,
XOXO. In my house, we sign off swords and shields. Is it a luxury to pick
battles like there will be one left to win? I like to pick a story. Go viral or go
yellow away under the mediocre off-white flag of the era we're calling hell.
Absorption over action equals erotic algebra, so master me in real time, in
zillions subscribed. You engineer a precedent and I'll give it legs that roam

mons and sinuous cables of Mars and all the moons. You be a sexual whiz
nuking the netherworld of our limbic system, your skin a deus ex machina
letting us live, at last—but we won't last. Let's bathe in screenglow as today
orbits a memory revolving around itself and you rewind you. Good headjob.
Kill, marry, or fuck me, me, or me? Let's sync and come to chimeric climax

pixel by pixel, let's fall to the cutting room floor. The script of the apocalyptic joyride leads to a new tryst in trilogy form where my body will, tomorrow, quit you. So I market you in red, flushed savior flaying the haunch of every id in a spitting fit of love. I want you to want me angry, naked, and ugly, perv reversing the life expectancy of an expectation, my purity to push to pulse. Heroes are what I want when I want it and by the bedside of my tableau substitutes unpeel from still shots I stashed to get me, compassionately, off. Gunmen defy gravity in the safe spaces even as your sex helps me hit *Eject*

The Weakest Link. I can't help feeling like something great is coming for me. White gunmen defy security everything every day for centuries until we can't see a thing. Let's not stop this, or weep. With enough engineering feeling becomes social intelligence and the upgrade is better, virtual as reality hitting home. You emulate loving something. I'll put my I down on a bed red and silken as a president's map dreaming big, tranq-washed between fine lines. The world can wait. I called the news I won a DJ contest and made him play our song. Let's go out with a bang, on a loop, xenon reddening the marquee of you and me before we lose my temper, OK, baby, it's OK, sort of. There's a national safety network for a pale concerto, your audience shooting children down, my fans jamming the rude signal. Are we there yet? This network put out a call for action. Let's make a clean zenith of that and wake up stars. Ever since I was a little girl, I had a dream.

Pastoral on Earth

Zoology counts us in (even in the –aughts) as against them
and against joining them, as not a fair choir but chimeras in

yellow moods, like a feral cat burying her fleas in the usual
bassinet; the overstretch of white geometry; the itching O;

xenocracy endangerous, for our alien tic is a diamond kick
cocked to outrun a calculus of human cocks, to go to sleep

worse and pray our sons be wild. A past the colony's judge
decorates with a princess-cut oath. If a vow has an IQ,

victory is color-blind: he can't "see" the scar under the lazuli
evening gown, "can't" imagine home in a biome of civil war

unless alienate women stimulate him to a maximal, toxic gush.
Future-feeder he. We were the old world but nothing is unless

terror blossoms a fist a cage force-fed, concentric rage a lung
grown in a meathouse, he a heart-shaped steak and we the root

sprouting a wing—watch for movement, a bomb of life. So if
holidays salivate, all the king's lions get in line, the impromptu

reverie regarding the gift of nature and the nature of gratitude.
If beaten with lust, we love else else our stripe flash on the TV,

questionable as a mouth of sand, bitter like a mouth of meat—
just like that, the cage door swings and flattens at the window

penetrated by arousal, and frames the nation as basically basic,
kings that flip the sodden cash of muscle as we unfarm our sex

over the wreck and the troubled, double helix of man—just a dab—
loitering here, a dear, glowing smear in the cavern we know why

no civilized road goes near. When we die, feed us to the flora
met in trenches. The germ may be forgiven. The bloomy, bloody fuzz.

The Alien Crown

My world, my world, its legendary grief, alive as a paper dragon
nesting or burning. I documented my life so am two worlds seam

-less and reeking of aping, of animal ashes, a *No* the state let go
off record. Fat reels of systemic fruit tumble in the feed to fill

kingdom and custom. My world full of agents, wired air. If I keep
passing to pass their test—planet without its star, an email stuck

just joking, a chain in plain sight—will I pass the interview? Q:
Quasi-queen, do you do real men? For an alien, wow. I saw and liked the Taj

in Agra. The wound is a world, its border longer than a river
rising ever, ebbing never, the bleed a reef in a hole. The origami

hell the inheritance of daughters who folded up in the wings
some life, real fury, no time. The utility of fire. As if it were flesh,

itself given to itself. Feed to it the sky, the shame, the testament
terrorized by its own dragon, actual children dying in the epilog.

The Alien Crown

Trouble exists—so drag on. Put down the paper beast of epilog
gone limp good night.
Flare to the legal system good night.

Under a narrative of stars, press at the world's first fence.
It's a chain, a fable of

fear in gold plating manufacturing
a life of feeling. No
more copies of you.

Voltas fail, but here we are, unhurt nowhere,
editing violence until we dawn.
The erotics of fear is a rich man's rev

wrenching you from your color. No more buying
anything in the end

despair took from compulsion. If not devotion,
not repression, its honorary white law

xenocratic in fair weather, its war undoing the stars, and worse, its magic

calling you *citizen*. Call it disaster,
your application to the world's index

yearning, and peel off the bloom of disguise like a woman from a tomb.

Be wordless with me, not
worldless. The anti-bomb when we choose to live, wildly

zero when we touch the world.

Call it home, a fable with no phobia

at all, where no house can keep us,

the dripping, golden hand that flies to the door
for birthright, this bliss against blitz.

Acknowledgments

Thank you to the editors of the following journals, in which poems from this book appeared: *A Poetry Congeries, APARTMENT Poetry, Better: Culture & Lit, Colorado Review, CURA: A Journal of Art and Action, Devil's Lake, Hayden's Ferry Review, jubilat, Los Angeles Review of Books, MiPOesias, New Orleans Review, Ninth Letter, PEN Poetry Series, Phoebe, Pinwheel, Poetry Northwest, Powder Keg, Sycamore Review, The Awl, The Margins, Third Coast,* and *Tongue.*

I am so grateful to Lesle Lewis, Shane McCrae, and Wendy Xu for choosing this book, and to Caryl Pagel for the humbling attention she gave it. Thank you to Clayton Adam Clark, Ally Day, and James Ellenberger for the thoughtful guidance you gave to these poems. As always, my gratitude goes to Kathy Fagan, for believing in me in the first place and still doing so. Thank you to every member of my Kundiman family, especially Sarah Gambito, Joseph Legaspi, and Cathy Linh Che. Kundiman forever. To my friends who wouldn't stop believing in me, my heart: Tonya Adams, Greg Alfred, Ally Day, Bill Heidrich, Brenna Ivey, Tina Jenkins, Emily Rock, and Nathan Thomas. And, always, my thanks to and for Jen Gable, without whom I wouldn't have gotten to this page.

I owe more to my family than can be bound. Thank you to my parents, James Kwa Boon Hwee and Brenda Wong Lai Ying, to my sister, Anna Kwa, to my grandparents, Kwa Chin Swee, Loh Siu Kee, Wong Veng Tim, and Koh Hwee Ngo, and, finally, to Elia Burkhart.

About the Author

Lo Kwa Mei-en is the author of *Yearling* (Alice James Books, 2015), winner of the Kundiman Poetry Prize, and two chapbooks, *The Romances* (The Lettered Streets Press) and *Two Tales* (Bloom Books). She lives and works in Cincinnati.